VEGETARIAN MEAL PLAN FOR BEGINNERS WITH

PRE DIABETES & HIGH CHOLESTEROL

Transform Your Health with Nutritious and Balanced Vegetarian

Recipes, Expertly Designed to Manage Prediabetes & High

Cholesterol

By Mia Bennett

TABLE OF CONTENTS

Chapter 3: Lunch Recipes 37

Chapter 4: Dinner Recipes 55

Chapter 5: Snacks and Appetizers 77

INTRODUCTION

I magine your body as a finely tuned engine. Pre-diabetes and high cholesterol are like warning lights on the dashboard, indicating potential trouble down the road. The good news? You can take control! This guide explores these conditions, the power of a plant-based diet, and strategies for a healthy future.

Understanding Pre-diabetes and High Cholesterol:

- **Pre-diabetes:** Your blood sugar levels are higher than normal, but not high enough for a type 2 diabetes diagnosis. Think of it as a chance to intervene and prevent the disease.
- **High Cholesterol:** This waxy substance builds up in arteries, increasing your risk of heart disease. There are two main culprits: LDL ("bad") cholesterol and HDL ("good") cholesterol. The goal is to lower LDL and raise HDL.

Why a Vegetarian Diet Can Be a Game Changer:

- **Fiber Powerhouse:** Plants are naturally packed with fiber, which helps regulate blood sugar and cholesterol. It keeps you feeling full and promotes gut health, a crucial factor in overall well-being.

- **Goodbye Saturated Fat:** Vegetarian meals tend to be lower in saturated fat, the primary villain behind high LDL cholesterol. Plant-based proteins like beans and lentils offer a healthy alternative.
- **A Rainbow on Your Plate:** Fruits and vegetables boast a vibrant array of vitamins, minerals, and antioxidants. These power players fight inflammation and support your body's natural defenses.

Key Nutrients to Focus On:

- **Soluble Fiber**: Found in oats, beans, and fruits like apples, it helps lower LDL cholesterol.
- **Healthy Fats:** Avocados, nuts, and seeds are rich in monounsaturated and polyunsaturated fats, promoting heart health.
- **Plant-Based Protein**: Beans, lentils, tofu, and tempeh provide essential protein while keeping saturated fat in check.
- **Vitamins and Minerals**: Leafy greens, colorful vegetables, and whole grains offer a treasure trove of these micronutrients, vital for overall health.

Tips for Meal Planning and Preparation:

- **Start Small:** Don't overwhelm yourself. Introduce one or two vegetarian meals a week and gradually increase.

- **Explore Ethnic Cuisines**: Vegetarian options abound in Indian, Thai, and Mediterranean dishes. Discover a world of flavor!

- **Prep is Key:** Wash and chop vegetables in advance for easy snacking and quick meals. Cook a large pot of lentil soup for lunches throughout the week.

- **Spice Up Your Life:** Experiment with herbs and spices to add variety and depth of flavor to your vegetarian dishes.

- **Make Friends with Leftovers:** Leftover lentil stew becomes a protein-packed salad or a filling wrap the next day. Reduce food waste and save time!

Remember: A vegetarian diet, combined with regular exercise, can be a powerful tool for managing pre-diabetes, lowering cholesterol, and promoting long-term health. It's about creating a sustainable lifestyle that nourishes your body and keeps that engine running smoothly!

Chapter 1: 30-Day Meal Plan

Week 1

Day 1

- Breakfast: Oatmeal with Fresh Berries and Nuts
- Lunch: Lentil Soup with Spinach
- Dinner: Stuffed Bell Peppers with Quinoa
- Snack: Roasted Chickpeas
- Dessert: Chia Seed Pudding with Fresh Berries

Day 2

- Breakfast: Greek Yogurt with Chia Seeds and Honey
- Lunch: Chickpea Salad with Cucumber and Tomatoes
- Dinner: Eggplant Parmesan
- Snack: Hummus with Carrot Sticks
- Dessert: Baked Pears with Cinnamon

Day 3

- Breakfast: Avocado Toast with Cherry Tomatoes
- Lunch: Quinoa and Black Bean Bowl
- Dinner: Vegetable Paella
- Snack: Guacamole with Whole Grain Crackers
- Dessert: Dark Chocolate and Almond Clusters

Day 4

- Breakfast: Veggie Omelette with Spinach and Mushrooms
- Lunch: Grilled Vegetable Sandwich
- Dinner: Spinach and Mushroom Lasagna
- Snack: Greek Yogurt with Fresh Berries
- Dessert: Mango Sorbet

Day 5

- Breakfast: Smoothie Bowl with Almond Butter
- Lunch: Spinach and Strawberry Salad with Walnuts
- Dinner: Lentil and Vegetable Stew
- Snack: Apple Slices with Peanut Butter
- Dessert: Apple Crisp with Oats

Day 6

- Breakfast: Whole Grain Pancakes with Blueberries
- Lunch: Vegetable Stir-Fry with Tofu
- Dinner: Baked Tofu with Vegetables
- Snack: Celery Sticks with Almond Butter
- Dessert: Blueberry Almond Parfait

Day 7

- Breakfast: Quinoa Breakfast Bowl with Almonds and Berries

- Lunch: Butternut Squash Soup
- Dinner: Chickpea and Spinach Curry
- Snack: Mixed Nuts and Seeds
- Dessert: Vegan Banana Bread

Week 2

Day 8

- Breakfast: Tofu Scramble with Bell Peppers
- Lunch: Mediterranean Hummus Wrap
- Dinner: Vegetable Kebabs with Brown Rice
- Snack: Edamame with Sea Salt
- Dessert: Coconut Milk Ice Cream

Day 9

- Breakfast: Overnight Chia Pudding with Mango
- Lunch: Broccoli and Almond Salad
- Dinner: Spaghetti Squash with Marinara
- Snack: Baked Kale Chips
- Dessert: Pumpkin Pie with Almond Crust

Day 10

- Breakfast: Spinach and Feta Breakfast Wrap
- Lunch: Cauliflower Rice with Peas and Carrots

- Dinner: Black Bean and Corn Enchiladas
- Snack: Stuffed Mini Bell Peppers
- Dessert: Raspberry Chia Jam Bars

Day 11

- Breakfast: Banana and Almond Butter Toast
- Lunch: Zucchini Noodles with Pesto
- Dinner: Cauliflower Pizza with Veggies
- Snack: Spicy Roasted Almonds
- Dessert: Avocado Chocolate Mousse

Day 12

- Breakfast: Cottage Cheese with Pineapple and Flax Seeds
- Lunch: Edamame and Avocado Salad
- Dinner: Thai Peanut Noodles with Vegetables
- Snack: Cottage Cheese with Cucumber Slices
- Dessert: Poached Pears with Spices

Day 13

- Breakfast: Buckwheat Porridge with Walnuts and Cinnamon
- Lunch: Red Lentil Curry
- Dinner: Moroccan Vegetable Tagine
- Snack: Berry and Nut Mix
- Dessert: Lemon Sorbet

Day 14

- Breakfast: Green Smoothie with Kale and Banana
- Lunch: Sweet Potato and Black Bean Tacos
- Dinner: Grilled Portobello Mushrooms
- Snack: Sliced Avocado with Lime
- Dessert: Strawberry Basil Popsicles

Week 3

Day 15

- Breakfast: Baked Apple with Cinnamon and Oats
- Lunch: Wild Rice and Mushroom Pilaf
- Dinner: Sweet Potato and Lentil Shepherd's Pie
- Snack: Tomato and Basil Bruschetta
- Dessert: Sweet Potato Brownies

Day 16

- Breakfast: Oatmeal with Fresh Berries and Nuts
- Lunch: Lentil Soup with Spinach
- Dinner: Stuffed Bell Peppers with Quinoa
- Snack: Roasted Chickpeas
- Dessert: Chia Seed Pudding with Fresh Berries

Day 17

- Breakfast: Greek Yogurt with Chia Seeds and Honey
- Lunch: Chickpea Salad with Cucumber and Tomatoes
- Dinner: Eggplant Parmesan
- Snack: Hummus with Carrot Sticks
- Dessert: Baked Pears with Cinnamon

Day 18

- Breakfast: Avocado Toast with Cherry Tomatoes
- Lunch: Quinoa and Black Bean Bowl
- Dinner: Vegetable Paella
- Snack: Guacamole with Whole Grain Crackers
- Dessert: Dark Chocolate and Almond Clusters

Day 19

- Breakfast: Veggie Omelette with Spinach and Mushrooms
- Lunch: Grilled Vegetable Sandwich
- Dinner: Spinach and Mushroom Lasagna
- Snack: Greek Yogurt with Fresh Berries
- Dessert: Mango Sorbet

Day 20

- Breakfast: Smoothie Bowl with Almond Butter
- Lunch: Spinach and Strawberry Salad with Walnuts

- Dinner: Lentil and Vegetable Stew
- Snack: Apple Slices with Peanut Butter
- Dessert: Apple Crisp with Oats

Day 21

- Breakfast: Whole Grain Pancakes with Blueberries
- Lunch: Vegetable Stir-Fry with Tofu
- Dinner: Baked Tofu with Vegetables
- Snack: Celery Sticks with Almond Butter
- Dessert: Blueberry Almond Parfait

Week 4

Day 22

- Breakfast: Quinoa Breakfast Bowl with Almonds and Berries
- Lunch: Butternut Squash Soup
- Dinner: Chickpea and Spinach Curry
- Snack: Mixed Nuts and Seeds
- Dessert: Vegan Banana Bread

Day 23

- Breakfast: Tofu Scramble with Bell Peppers
- Lunch: Mediterranean Hummus Wrap

- Dinner: Vegetable Kebabs with Brown Rice
- Snack: Edamame with Sea Salt
- Dessert: Coconut Milk Ice Cream

Day 24

- Breakfast: Overnight Chia Pudding with Mango
- Lunch: Broccoli and Almond Salad
- Dinner: Spaghetti Squash with Marinara
- Snack: Baked Kale Chips
- Dessert: Pumpkin Pie with Almond Crust

Day 25

- Breakfast: Spinach and Feta Breakfast Wrap
- Lunch: Cauliflower Rice with Peas and Carrots
- Dinner: Black Bean and Corn Enchiladas
- Snack: Stuffed Mini Bell Peppers
- Dessert: Raspberry Chia Jam Bars

Day 26

- Breakfast: Banana and Almond Butter Toast
- Lunch: Zucchini Noodles with Pesto
- Dinner: Cauliflower Pizza with Veggies
- Snack: Spicy Roasted Almonds
- Dessert: Avocado Chocolate Mousse

Day 27

- Breakfast: Cottage Cheese with Pineapple and Flax Seeds
- Lunch: Edamame and Avocado Salad
- Dinner: Thai Peanut Noodles with Vegetables
- Snack: Cottage Cheese with Cucumber Slices
- Dessert: Poached Pears with Spices

Day 28

- Breakfast: Buckwheat Porridge with Walnuts and Cinnamon
- Lunch: Red Lentil Curry
- Dinner: Moroccan Vegetable Tagine
- Snack: Berry and Nut Mix
- Dessert: Lemon Sorbet

Day 29

- Breakfast: Green Smoothie with Kale and Banana
- Lunch: Sweet Potato and Black Bean Tacos
- Dinner: Grilled Portobello Mushrooms
- Snack: Sliced Avocado with Lime
- Dessert: Strawberry Basil Popsicles

Day 30

- Breakfast: Baked Apple with Cinnamon and Oats
- Lunch: Wild Rice and Mushroom Pilaf

- Dinner: Sweet Potato and Lentil Shepherd's Pie
- Snack: Tomato and Basil Bruschetta
- Dessert: Sweet Potato Brownies

Chapter 2: Breakfast Recipes

Starting your day with a nutritious breakfast can set the tone for healthy eating habits throughout the day. These breakfast recipes are designed to be not only delicious but also beneficial for managing pre-diabetes and high cholesterol. Each recipe focuses on using wholesome, plant-based ingredients to provide balanced nutrition.

Oatmeal with Fresh Berries and Nuts

Ingredients:

- 1 cup rolled oats
- 2 cups water or almond milk
- 1/2 cup mixed fresh berries (strawberries, blueberries, raspberries)
- 1/4 cup chopped nuts (almonds, walnuts)
- 1 tbsp honey (optional)

Instructions:

1. Bring water or almond milk to a boil in a pot.
2. Add oats and reduce heat to simmer for 5-7 minutes.
3. Top with fresh berries and nuts.
4. Drizzle with honey if desired.

Nutrition Information (per serving):

- Calories: 350
- Protein: 9g
- Carbohydrates: 55g
- Fat: 12g
- Fiber: 8g
- Sugar: 12g
- Portion Size: 1 bowl

Greek Yogurt with Chia Seeds and Honey

Ingredients:

- 1 cup Greek yogurt
- 1 tbsp chia seeds
- 1 tbsp honey
- 1/4 cup sliced almonds

Instructions:

1. Mix Greek yogurt with chia seeds.
2. Drizzle honey over the top.
3. Sprinkle with sliced almonds.

Nutrition Information (per serving):

- Calories: 250

- Protein: 15g
- Carbohydrates: 20g
- Fat: 10g
- Fiber: 5g
- Sugar: 15g
- Portion Size: 1 cup

Avocado Toast with Cherry Tomatoes

Ingredients:

- 1 slice whole grain bread
- 1/2 avocado
- 1/4 cup cherry tomatoes, halved
- Salt and pepper to taste

Instructions:

1. Toast the bread.
2. Mash avocado and spread on toast.
3. Top with cherry tomatoes.
4. Season with salt and pepper.

Nutrition Information (per serving):

- Calories: 220
- Protein: 4g

- Carbohydrates: 24g
- Fat: 14g
- Fiber: 8g
- Sugar: 2g
- Portion Size: 1 toast

Veggie Omelette with Spinach and Mushrooms

Ingredients:

- 2 eggs
- 1/4 cup spinach, chopped
- 1/4 cup mushrooms, sliced
- 1 tbsp olive oil
- Salt and pepper to taste

Instructions:

1. Whisk eggs in a bowl.
2. Heat olive oil in a pan over medium heat.
3. Sauté spinach and mushrooms until tender.
4. Pour eggs over vegetables and cook until set.
5. Season with salt and pepper.

Nutrition Information (per serving):

- Calories: 200
- Protein: 14g
- Carbohydrates: 4g
- Fat: 14g
- Fiber: 1g
- Sugar: 1g
- Portion Size: 1 omelette

Smoothie Bowl with Almond Butter

Ingredients:

- 1 banana
- 1/2 cup frozen berries
- 1/2 cup almond milk
- 1 tbsp almond butter
- 1 tbsp chia seeds

Instructions:

1. Blend banana, berries, and almond milk until smooth.
2. Pour into a bowl.
3. Top with almond butter and chia seeds.

Nutrition Information (per serving):

- Calories: 300
- Protein: 7g
- Carbohydrates: 45g
- Fat: 12g
- Fiber: 8g
- Sugar: 20g
- Portion Size: 1 bowl

Whole Grain Pancakes with Blueberries

Ingredients:

- 1 cup whole grain flour
- 1 cup almond milk
- 1 egg
- 1 tsp baking powder
- 1/2 cup fresh blueberries

Instructions:

1. Mix flour, almond milk, egg, and baking powder in a bowl.
2. Fold in blueberries.
3. Cook pancakes on a heated griddle until golden brown.

Nutrition Information (per serving):

- Calories: 250
- Protein: 8g
- Carbohydrates: 40g
- Fat: 6g
- Fiber: 6g
- Sugar: 10g
- Portion Size: 3 pancakes

Quinoa Breakfast Bowl with Almonds and Berries

Ingredients:

- 1 cup cooked quinoa
- 1/2 cup almond milk
- 1/4 cup fresh berries
- 2 tbsp sliced almonds
- 1 tbsp honey (optional)

Instructions:

1. Mix cooked quinoa with almond milk.
2. Top with fresh berries and sliced almonds.
3. Drizzle with honey if desired.

Nutrition Information (per serving):

- Calories: 300
- Protein: 8g
- Carbohydrates: 45g
- Fat: 10g
- Fiber: 6g
- Sugar: 15g
- Portion Size: 1 bowl

Tofu Scramble with Bell Peppers

Ingredients:

- 1/2 block firm tofu, crumbled
- 1/4 cup bell peppers, diced
- 1 tbsp olive oil
- 1/2 tsp turmeric
- Salt and pepper to taste

Instructions:

1. Heat olive oil in a pan over medium heat.
2. Add bell peppers and sauté until tender.
3. Add crumbled tofu and turmeric, cook for 5 minutes.
4. Season with salt and pepper.

Nutrition Information (per serving):

- Calories: 180
- Protein: 12g
- Carbohydrates: 6g
- Fat: 12g
- Fiber: 2g
- Sugar: 2g
- Portion Size: 1 scramble

Overnight Chia Pudding with Mango

Ingredients:

- 1/4 cup chia seeds
- 1 cup almond milk
- 1/2 mango, diced

Instructions:

1. Mix chia seeds with almond milk in a jar.
2. Refrigerate overnight.
3. Top with diced mango before serving.

Nutrition Information (per serving):

- Calories: 250
- Protein: 6g

- Carbohydrates: 28g
- Fat: 12g
- Fiber: 10g
- Sugar: 18g
- Portion Size: 1 jar

Spinach and Feta Breakfast Wrap

Ingredients:

- 1 whole grain tortilla
- 1/2 cup spinach, chopped
- 1/4 cup feta cheese
- 1 egg
- 1 tbsp olive oil

Instructions:

1. Scramble egg in a pan with olive oil.
2. Add spinach and cook until wilted.
3. Place scrambled egg and spinach on tortilla.
4. Sprinkle with feta cheese and wrap.

Nutrition Information (per serving):

- Calories: 300
- Protein: 12g

- Carbohydrates: 28g
- Fat: 16g
- Fiber: 4g
- Sugar: 2g
- Portion Size: 1 wrap

Banana and Almond Butter Toast

Ingredients:
- 1 slice whole grain bread
- 1 tbsp almond butter
- 1/2 banana, sliced

Instructions:
1. Toast the bread.
2. Spread almond butter on toast.
3. Top with banana slices.

Nutrition Information (per serving):
- Calories: 220
- Protein: 5g
- Carbohydrates: 30g
- Fat: 10g
- Fiber: 5g

- Sugar: 12g
- Portion Size: 1 toast

Cottage Cheese with Pineapple and Flax Seeds

Ingredients:
- 1 cup cottage cheese
- 1/2 cup pineapple chunks
- 1 tbsp flax seeds

Instructions:
1. Mix cottage cheese with pineapple chunks.
2. Sprinkle with flax seeds.

Nutrition Information (per serving):
- Calories: 200
- Protein: 14g
- Carbohydrates: 18g
- Fat: 6g
- Fiber: 4g
- Sugar: 10g
- Portion Size: 1 cup

Buckwheat Porridge with Walnuts and Cinnamon

Ingredients:

- 1 cup buckwheat groats
- 2 cups water
- 1/4 cup walnuts, chopped
- 1 tsp cinnamon

Instructions:

1. Bring water to a boil and add buckwheat groats.
2. Reduce heat and simmer for 15 minutes.
3. Top with walnuts and sprinkle with cinnamon.

Nutrition Information (per serving):

- Calories: 300
- Protein: 10g
- Carbohydrates: 50g
- Fat: 10g
- Fiber: 8g
- Sugar: 2g
- Portion Size: 1 bowl

Green Smoothie with Kale and Banana

Ingredients:

- 1 banana
- 1 cup kale leaves
- 1 cup almond milk
- 1 tbsp chia seeds

Instructions:

1. Blend banana, kale, and almond milk until smooth.
2. Pour into a glass.
3. Stir in chia seeds.

Nutrition Information (per serving):

- Calories: 200
- Protein: 5g
- Carbohydrates: 30g
- Fat: 8g
- Fiber: 6g
- Sugar: 15g
- Portion Size: 1 glass

Baked Apple with Cinnamon and Oats

Ingredients:

- 1 apple
- 1 tbsp oats
- 1 tsp cinnamon
- 1 tbsp honey

Instructions:

1. Core the apple and fill with oats and cinnamon.
2. Drizzle with honey.
3. Bake at 350°F for 20 minutes.

Nutrition Information (per serving):

- Calories: 150
- Protein: 1g
- Carbohydrates: 38g
- Fat: 1g
- Fiber: 5g
- Sugar: 30g
- Portion Size: 1 apple

Chapter 3: Lunch Recipes

Creating a meal plan for individuals with pre-diabetes and high cholesterol can be both delicious and nutritious. This chapter focuses on lunch recipes that are balanced, heart-healthy, and easy to prepare. Each recipe is designed to provide essential nutrients without spiking blood sugar levels or increasing cholesterol. Here are satisfying and healthy lunch recipes to enjoy.

Lentil Soup with Spinach

Ingredients:

- 1 cup lentils, rinsed
- 1 onion, diced
- 2 carrots, diced
- 2 celery stalks, diced
- 2 garlic cloves, minced
- 1 can diced tomatoes
- 4 cups vegetable broth
- 2 cups spinach leaves
- 1 tsp cumin
- 1 tsp paprika
- Salt and pepper to taste

Instructions:

1. In a large pot, sauté onion, carrots, celery, and garlic until softened.
2. Add lentils, diced tomatoes, and vegetable broth.
3. Season with cumin, paprika, salt, and pepper.
4. Bring to a boil, then reduce heat and simmer for 30 minutes.
5. Stir in spinach leaves until wilted.

Nutrition Information:

- Calories: 200
- Protein: 12g
- Carbohydrates: 35g
- Fat: 2g
- Fiber: 15g
- Sugar: 6g
- Portion Size: 1 bowl (about 2 cups)

Chickpea Salad with Cucumber and Tomatoes

Ingredients:

- 1 can chickpeas, drained and rinsed
- 1 cucumber, diced
- 2 tomatoes, diced

- 1/4 red onion, thinly sliced
- 2 tbsp olive oil
- 1 tbsp lemon juice
- 1 tsp dried oregano
- Salt and pepper to taste

Instructions:

1. Combine chickpeas, cucumber, tomatoes, and red onion in a bowl.
2. In a small bowl, whisk together olive oil, lemon juice, oregano, salt, and pepper.
3. Pour dressing over salad and toss to combine.

Nutrition Information:

- Calories: 220
- Protein: 7g
- Carbohydrates: 28g
- Fat: 10g
- Fiber: 8g
- Sugar: 5g
- Portion Size: 1 cup

Quinoa and Black Bean Bowl

Ingredients:

- 1 cup quinoa, rinsed
- 1 can black beans, drained and rinsed
- 1 cup corn kernels
- 1 red bell pepper, diced
- 1 avocado, diced
- 1/4 cup cilantro, chopped
- 2 tbsp lime juice
- Salt and pepper to taste

Instructions:

1. Cook quinoa according to package instructions.
2. In a large bowl, combine cooked quinoa, black beans, corn, bell pepper, avocado, and cilantro.
3. Drizzle with lime juice, and season with salt and pepper. Toss to combine.

Nutrition Information:

- Calories: 350
- Protein: 12g
- Carbohydrates: 55g
- Fat: 10g
- Fiber: 14g

- Sugar: 5g
- Portion Size: 1 bowl (about 1.5 cups)

Grilled Vegetable Sandwich

Ingredients:

- 1 zucchini, sliced
- 1 red bell pepper, sliced
- 1 eggplant, sliced
- 2 tbsp olive oil
- 4 whole-grain sandwich rolls
- 1/4 cup hummus
- Handful of arugula
- Salt and pepper to taste

Instructions:

1. Brush zucchini, bell pepper, and eggplant slices with olive oil, and season with salt and pepper.
2. Grill vegetables until tender.
3. Spread hummus on sandwich rolls.
4. Layer grilled vegetables and arugula on the rolls.

Nutrition Information:

- Calories: 320

- Protein: 8g
- Carbohydrates: 45g
- Fat: 12g
- Fiber: 9g
- Sugar: 8g
- Portion Size: 1 sandwich

Spinach and Strawberry Salad with Walnuts

Ingredients:
- 4 cups baby spinach
- 1 cup strawberries, sliced
- 1/4 cup walnuts, chopped
- 2 tbsp balsamic vinaigrette

Instructions:
1. In a large bowl, combine spinach, strawberries, and walnuts.
2. Drizzle with balsamic vinaigrette and toss gently to combine.

Nutrition Information:
- Calories: 150
- Protein: 3g

- Carbohydrates: 14g
- Fat: 10g
- Fiber: 4g
- Sugar: 8g
- Portion Size: 1 bowl (about 2 cups)

Vegetable Stir-Fry with Tofu

Ingredients:
- 1 block firm tofu, cubed
- 1 tbsp olive oil
- 1 red bell pepper, sliced
- 1 yellow bell pepper, sliced
- 1 cup broccoli florets
- 2 garlic cloves, minced
- 1 tbsp soy sauce
- 1 tbsp hoisin sauce

Instructions:
1. Heat olive oil in a pan and sauté tofu cubes until golden brown. Remove and set aside.
2. In the same pan, sauté bell peppers, broccoli, and garlic until tender.

3. Add tofu back to the pan and stir in soy sauce and hoisin sauce.

Nutrition Information:
- Calories: 250
- Protein: 15g
- Carbohydrates: 18g
- Fat: 14g
- Fiber: 6g
- Sugar: 6g
- Portion Size: 1 bowl (about 1.5 cups)

Butternut Squash Soup

Ingredients:
- 1 butternut squash, peeled and cubed
- 1 onion, diced
- 2 garlic cloves, minced
- 4 cups vegetable broth
- 1 tsp thyme
- 1/2 cup coconut milk
- Salt and pepper to taste

Instructions:

1. In a large pot, sauté onion and garlic until fragrant.

2. Add butternut squash and vegetable broth. Bring to a boil.

3. Reduce heat and simmer until squash is tender.

4. Blend soup until smooth, then stir in thyme, coconut milk, salt, and pepper.

Nutrition Information:

- Calories: 180
- Protein: 2g
- Carbohydrates: 30g
- Fat: 6g
- Fiber: 5g
- Sugar: 7g
- Portion Size: 1 bowl (about 2 cups)

Mediterranean Hummus Wrap

Ingredients:

- 4 whole-grain tortillas
- 1 cup hummus
- 1 cucumber, sliced
- 1 tomato, sliced
- 1/4 cup kalamata olives, sliced

- 1/4 cup feta cheese, crumbled
- Handful of spinach

Instructions:

1. Spread hummus on each tortilla.
2. Layer with cucumber, tomato, olives, feta cheese, and spinach.
3. Roll up the tortillas and slice in half.

Nutrition Information:

- Calories: 320
- Protein: 8g
- Carbohydrates: 38g
- Fat: 14g
- Fiber: 8g
- Sugar: 4g
- Portion Size: 1 wrap

Broccoli and Almond Salad

Ingredients:

- 2 cups broccoli florets
- 1/4 cup sliced almonds
- 1/4 cup dried cranberries

- 2 tbsp olive oil
- 1 tbsp apple cider vinegar
- Salt and pepper to taste

Instructions:

1. In a large bowl, combine broccoli, almonds, and cranberries.
2. In a small bowl, whisk together olive oil, apple cider vinegar, salt, and pepper.
3. Pour dressing over salad and toss to combine.

Nutrition Information:

- Calories: 180
- Protein: 4g
- Carbohydrates: 15g
- Fat: 12g
- Fiber: 5g
- Sugar: 7g
- Portion Size: 1 cup

Cauliflower Rice with Peas and Carrots

Ingredients:

- 1 head cauliflower, grated into rice-sized pieces
- 1 cup peas

- 1 cup diced carrots
- 2 garlic cloves, minced
- 1 tbsp olive oil
- 2 tbsp soy sauce

Instructions:

1. Heat olive oil in a pan and sauté garlic until fragrant.
2. Add cauliflower rice, peas, and carrots, and cook until tender.
3. Stir in soy sauce and cook for an additional 2 minutes.

Nutrition Information:

- Calories: 130
- Protein: 4g
- Carbohydrates: 20g
- Fat: 4g
- Fiber: 6g
- Sugar: 5g
- Portion Size: 1 cup

Zucchini Noodles with Pesto

Ingredients:

- 2 zucchinis, spiralized into noodles

- 1/4 cup pesto
- 1/2 cup cherry tomatoes, halved
- 1/4 cup pine nuts

Instructions:

1. In a large bowl, toss zucchini noodles with pesto until well coated.
2. Add cherry tomatoes and pine nuts, and toss to combine.

Nutrition Information:
- Calories: 180
- Protein: 5g
- Carbohydrates: 10g
- Fat: 14g
- Fiber: 3g
- Sugar: 4g
- Portion Size: 1 bowl (about 2 cups)

Edamame and Avocado Salad

Ingredients:
- 1 cup shelled edamame
- 1 avocado, diced
- 1/2 red onion, diced

- 1 tbsp olive oil
- 1 tbsp lemon juice
- Salt and pepper to taste

Instructions:

1. In a large bowl, combine edamame, avocado, and red onion.
2. Drizzle with olive oil and lemon juice, and season with salt and pepper. Toss gently to combine.

Nutrition Information:

- Calories: 240
- Protein: 9g
- Carbohydrates: 16g
- Fat: 18g
- Fiber: 8g
- Sugar: 2g
- Portion Size: 1 bowl (about 1.5 cups)

Red Lentil Curry

Ingredients:

- 1 cup red lentils, rinsed
- 1 onion, diced
- 2 garlic cloves, minced

- 1 can coconut milk
- 2 cups vegetable broth
- 1 tbsp curry powder
- 1 tsp turmeric
- 1 tsp cumin
- Salt and pepper to taste

Instructions:
1. In a large pot, sauté onion and garlic until softened.
2. Add red lentils, coconut milk, vegetable broth, curry powder, turmeric, cumin, salt, and pepper.
3. Bring to a boil, then reduce heat and simmer for 20 minutes until lentils are tender.

Nutrition Information:
- Calories: 270
- Protein: 13g
- Carbohydrates: 36g
- Fat: 9g
- Fiber: 12g
- Sugar: 4g
- Portion Size: 1 bowl (about 2 cups)

Sweet Potato and Black Bean Tacos

Ingredients:

- 2 sweet potatoes, diced
- 1 can black beans, drained and rinsed
- 1 tbsp olive oil
- 1 tsp cumin
- 1 tsp paprika
- 8 small corn tortillas
- 1/4 cup cilantro, chopped

Instructions:

1. Toss sweet potatoes with olive oil, cumin, and paprika. Roast at 400°F for 20 minutes.
2. In a bowl, combine roasted sweet potatoes and black beans.
3. Warm tortillas and fill with sweet potato mixture. Top with cilantro.

Nutrition Information:

- Calories: 320
- Protein: 8g
- Carbohydrates: 58g
- Fat: 6g
- Fiber: 12g
- Sugar: 7g

- Portion Size: 2 tacos

Wild Rice and Mushroom Pilaf

Ingredients:

- 1 cup wild rice, rinsed
- 2 cups vegetable broth
- 1 cup mushrooms, sliced
- 1 onion, diced
- 2 garlic cloves, minced
- 2 tbsp olive oil
- 1 tsp thyme
- Salt and pepper to taste

Instructions:

1. Cook wild rice in vegetable broth according to package instructions.
2. In a pan, sauté onion, garlic, and mushrooms in olive oil until tender.
3. Stir in cooked wild rice and thyme. Season with salt and pepper.

Nutrition Information:

- Calories: 250

- Protein: 6g
- Carbohydrates: 40g
- Fat: 8g
- Fiber: 5g
- Sugar: 3g
- Portion Size: 1 bowl (about 1.5 cups)

Chapter 4: Dinner Recipes

In this chapter, explore a variety of wholesome vegetarian dinner recipes that are delicious and tailored for those managing pre-diabetes and high cholesterol. Each recipe focuses on nutrient-dense ingredients to support a balanced diet.

Stuffed Bell Peppers with Quinoa

Ingredients:

- 4 large bell peppers, any color
- 1 cup quinoa, cooked
- 1 can black beans, rinsed and drained
- 1 cup corn kernels
- 1 cup diced tomatoes
- 1 teaspoon cumin
- 1 teaspoon chili powder
- Salt and pepper to taste
- Fresh cilantro for garnish

Instructions:

1. Preheat oven to 375°F (190°C). Cut the tops off the bell peppers and remove seeds.

2. In a bowl, mix cooked quinoa, black beans, corn, diced tomatoes, cumin, chili powder, salt, and pepper.
3. Stuff each bell pepper with the quinoa mixture.
4. Place stuffed peppers in a baking dish and cover with foil. Bake for 25-30 minutes until peppers are tender.
5. Garnish with fresh cilantro before serving.

Nutrition Information:

- Calories: 320
- Protein: 12g
- Carbohydrates: 62g
- Fat: 3g
- Fiber: 12g
- Sugar: 8g
- Portion Size: 1 stuffed pepper

Eggplant Parmesan

Ingredients:

- 2 large eggplants, sliced into rounds
- 1 cup whole wheat breadcrumbs
- 1 cup grated Parmesan cheese
- 2 cups marinara sauce
- 1 cup part-skim mozzarella cheese, shredded

- Fresh basil leaves for garnish

Instructions:

1. Preheat oven to 375°F (190°C). Place eggplant slices on a baking sheet and bake for 15 minutes until tender.
2. In a shallow dish, mix breadcrumbs and Parmesan cheese. Dip each eggplant slice into the mixture to coat.
3. In a baking dish, spread a layer of marinara sauce. Arrange a layer of coated eggplant slices on top. Repeat layers, finishing with marinara sauce.
4. Sprinkle mozzarella cheese on top. Cover with foil and bake for 25 minutes. Remove foil and bake for an additional 10 minutes until cheese is melted and bubbly.
5. Garnish with fresh basil leaves before serving.

Nutrition Information:
- Calories: 380
- Protein: 18g
- Carbohydrates: 45g
- Fat: 14g
- Fiber: 12g
- Sugar: 15g
- Portion Size: 1/6 of the dish

Vegetable Paella

Ingredients:

- 1 cup Arborio rice
- 2 cups vegetable broth
- 1 onion, diced
- 2 cloves garlic, minced
- 1 red bell pepper, sliced
- 1 yellow bell pepper, sliced
- 1 cup frozen peas
- 1 cup diced tomatoes
- 1 teaspoon smoked paprika
- 1/2 teaspoon saffron threads (optional)
- Salt and pepper to taste
- Fresh parsley for garnish

Instructions:

1. In a large skillet, sauté onion and garlic until softened.
2. Add sliced bell peppers and cook until tender.
3. Stir in Arborio rice, diced tomatoes, smoked paprika, and saffron threads (if using). Cook for 1-2 minutes.
4. Pour in vegetable broth and bring to a simmer. Cover and cook for 20 minutes until rice is tender and liquid is absorbed.

5. Stir in frozen peas and cook for an additional 5 minutes until heated through.

6. Season with salt and pepper. Garnish with fresh parsley before serving.

Nutrition Information:
- Calories: 320
- Protein: 8g
- Carbohydrates: 68g
- Fat: 2g
- Fiber: 8g
- Sugar: 8g
- Portion Size: 1/4 of the dish

Spinach and Mushroom Lasagna

Ingredients:
- 9 lasagna noodles, cooked according to package instructions
- 2 cups spinach, chopped
- 2 cups mushrooms, sliced
- 2 cups ricotta cheese
- 2 cups marinara sauce
- 1 cup part-skim mozzarella cheese, shredded
- 1/2 cup grated Parmesan cheese

- Fresh basil leaves for garnish

Instructions:

1. Preheat oven to 375°F (190°C). In a skillet, sauté spinach and mushrooms until softened.
2. In a large bowl, mix ricotta cheese with sautéed spinach and mushrooms.
3. Spread a layer of marinara sauce in a baking dish. Arrange a layer of cooked lasagna noodles on top.
4. Spread half of the ricotta mixture over the noodles. Repeat layers, finishing with marinara sauce.
5. Sprinkle mozzarella and Parmesan cheese on top. Cover with foil and bake for 30 minutes.
6. Remove foil and bake for an additional 10 minutes until cheese is golden and bubbly.
7. Garnish with fresh basil leaves before serving.

Nutrition Information:

- Calories: 420
- Protein: 25g
- Carbohydrates: 45g
- Fat: 18g
- Fiber: 5g
- Sugar: 8g

- Portion Size: 1/6 of the dish

Lentil and Vegetable Stew

Ingredients:

- 1 cup green lentils, rinsed
- 4 cups vegetable broth
- 1 onion, diced
- 2 carrots, diced
- 2 celery stalks, diced
- 2 cloves garlic, minced
- 1 teaspoon dried thyme
- 1 teaspoon dried rosemary
- Salt and pepper to taste
- Fresh parsley for garnish

Instructions:

1. In a large pot, sauté onion, carrots, celery, and garlic until softened.
2. Add green lentils, vegetable broth, dried thyme, and dried rosemary. Bring to a boil.
3. Reduce heat, cover, and simmer for 30-35 minutes until lentils are tender.
4. Season with salt and pepper to taste.

5. Garnish with fresh parsley before serving.

Nutrition Information:

- Calories: 280
- Protein: 16g
- Carbohydrates: 48g
- Fat: 1g
- Fiber: 18g
- Sugar: 6g
- Portion Size: 1/4 of the stew

Baked Tofu with Vegetables

Ingredients:

- 1 block tofu, pressed and cubed
- 2 tablespoons soy sauce
- 1 tablespoon olive oil
- 1 teaspoon garlic powder
- 1 teaspoon smoked paprika
- 2 cups mixed vegetables (broccoli, bell peppers, zucchini)
- Salt and pepper to taste
- Sesame seeds for garnish

Instructions:

1. Preheat oven to 400°F (200°C). In a bowl, toss cubed tofu with soy sauce, olive oil, garlic powder, and smoked paprika.

2. Arrange tofu on a baking sheet lined with parchment paper. Bake for 20-25 minutes until tofu is golden and crispy.

3. In the meantime, toss mixed vegetables with olive oil, salt, and pepper. Spread them on a separate baking sheet and roast for 15-20 minutes until tender.

4. Serve baked tofu with roasted vegetables, garnished with sesame seeds.

Nutrition Information:

- Calories: 320
- Protein: 20g
- Carbohydrates: 20g
- Fat: 18g
- Fiber: 8g
- Sugar: 6g
- Portion Size: 1/4 of the dish

Chickpea and Spinach Curry

Ingredients:

- 1 can chickpeas, rinsed and drained

- 1 onion, diced
- 2 cloves garlic, minced
- 1 tablespoon curry powder
- 1 teaspoon ground turmeric
- 1 can coconut milk
- 2 cups fresh spinach
- Salt and pepper to taste
- Fresh cilantro for garnish

Instructions:

1. In a large skillet, sauté onion and garlic until softened.
2. Add curry powder and turmeric, stirring for 1 minute until fragrant.
3. Stir in chickpeas and coconut milk. Bring to a simmer and cook for 10 minutes.
4. Add fresh spinach and cook until wilted.
5. Season with salt and pepper to taste.
6. Garnish with fresh cilantro before serving.

Nutrition Information:

- Calories: 380
- Protein: 12g
- Carbohydrates: 30g
- Fat: 25g

- Fiber: 8g
- Sugar: 6g
- Portion Size: 1/4 of the curry

Vegetable Kebabs with Brown Rice

Ingredients:
- 2 bell peppers, cut into chunks
- 1 zucchini, sliced
- 1 red onion, cut into wedges
- 8 cherry tomatoes
- 8 button mushrooms
- 2 tablespoons olive oil
- 1 tablespoon balsamic vinegar
- 1 teaspoon dried oregano
- Salt and pepper to taste
- Cooked brown rice for serving

Instructions:
1. Preheat grill or grill pan over medium-high heat.
2. In a bowl, toss bell peppers, zucchini, red onion, cherry tomatoes, and mushrooms with olive oil, balsamic vinegar, dried oregano, salt, and pepper.
3. Thread vegetables onto skewers, alternating varieties.

4. Grill kebabs for 10-15 minutes, turning occasionally, until vegetables are tender and lightly charred.

5. Serve vegetable kebabs over cooked brown rice.

Nutrition Information:

- Calories: 280
- Protein: 6g
- Carbohydrates: 40g
- Fat: 10g
- Fiber: 8g
- Sugar: 10g
- Portion Size: 1/4 of the kebabs with rice

Spaghetti Squash with Marinara

Ingredients:

- 1 spaghetti squash
- 2 cups marinara sauce (store-bought or homemade)
- 1 tablespoon olive oil
- 2 cloves garlic, minced
- 1/2 teaspoon dried basil
- 1/2 teaspoon dried oregano
- Salt and pepper to taste
- Fresh parsley for garnish

Instructions:

1. Preheat oven to 400°F (200°C). Cut spaghetti squash in half lengthwise and scoop out seeds.

2. Brush cut sides with olive oil and place squash halves, cut-side down, on a baking sheet.

3. Bake for 40-50 minutes until squash is tender and easily pierced with a fork.

4. In a skillet, sauté garlic in olive oil until fragrant. Add marinara sauce, dried basil, dried oregano, salt, and pepper. Simmer for 5 minutes.

5. Scrape the flesh of the cooked spaghetti squash with a fork to create "spaghetti" strands.

6. Serve spaghetti squash topped with marinara sauce. Garnish with fresh parsley before serving.

Nutrition Information:

- Calories: 220
- Protein: 4g
- Carbohydrates: 40g
- Fat: 8g
- Fiber: 10g
- Sugar: 12g
- Portion Size: 1/2 of the squash with sauce

Black Bean and Corn Enchiladas

Ingredients:

- 1 can black beans, rinsed and drained
- 1 cup corn kernels
- 1 red bell pepper, diced
- 1/2 cup diced red onion
- 1 teaspoon ground cumin
- 1/2 teaspoon chili powder
- 1 cup enchilada sauce (store-bought or homemade)
- 8 whole wheat tortillas
- 1 cup shredded Mexican cheese blend
- Fresh cilantro for garnish

Instructions:

1. Preheat oven to 375°F (190°C). In a bowl, mix black beans, corn, red bell pepper, red onion, ground cumin, and chili powder.
2. Pour a small amount of enchilada sauce into the bottom of a baking dish.
3. Spoon bean and vegetable mixture into each tortilla, roll up, and place seam-side down in the baking dish.
4. Pour remaining enchilada sauce over the top. Sprinkle with shredded cheese.

5. Cover with foil and bake for 20 minutes. Remove foil and bake for an additional 10 minutes until cheese is melted and bubbly.
6. Garnish with fresh cilantro before serving.

Nutrition Information:
- Calories: 350
- Protein: 15g
- Carbohydrates: 50g
- Fat: 12g
- Fiber: 10g
- Sugar: 8g
- Portion Size: 2 enchiladas

Cauliflower Pizza with Veggies

Ingredients:
- 1 cauliflower pizza crust (store-bought or homemade)
- 1 cup marinara sauce
- 1 cup shredded mozzarella cheese
- 1 cup assorted vegetables (bell peppers, mushrooms, spinach)
- 1 tablespoon olive oil
- Salt and pepper to taste

- Fresh basil leaves for garnish

Instructions:

1. Preheat oven according to cauliflower crust package instructions.
2. Spread marinara sauce evenly over the cauliflower crust.
3. Sprinkle shredded mozzarella cheese over the sauce.
4. Toss assorted vegetables with olive oil, salt, and pepper. Arrange them evenly over the pizza.
5. Bake according to cauliflower crust package instructions until cheese is melted and crust is crisp.
6. Garnish with fresh basil leaves before serving.

Nutrition Information:

- Calories: 280
- Protein: 15g
- Carbohydrates: 25g
- Fat: 14g
- Fiber: 8g
- Sugar: 6g
- Portion Size: 1/2 of the pizza

Thai Peanut Noodles with Vegetables

Ingredients:

- 8 oz rice noodles, cooked according to package instructions
- 1 cup mixed vegetables (bell peppers, carrots, snap peas)
- 1/2 cup shredded cabbage
- 1/4 cup creamy peanut butter
- 2 tablespoons soy sauce
- 1 tablespoon rice vinegar
- 1 tablespoon honey or agave syrup
- 1 clove garlic, minced
- 1 teaspoon grated ginger
- Crushed peanuts and sliced green onions for garnish

Instructions:

1. In a large skillet or wok, sauté mixed vegetables and shredded cabbage until tender-crisp.
2. In a bowl, whisk together peanut butter, soy sauce, rice vinegar, honey or agave syrup, garlic, and ginger until smooth.
3. Add cooked rice noodles and peanut sauce to the skillet. Toss to combine and heat through.
4. Serve Thai peanut noodles garnished with crushed peanuts and sliced green onions.

Nutrition Information:

- Calories: 380

- Protein: 10g

- Carbohydrates: 60g

- Fat: 12g

- Fiber: 6g

- Sugar: 8g

- Portion Size: 1/4 of the recipe

Moroccan Vegetable Tagine

Ingredients:

- 1 onion, diced

- 2 cloves garlic, minced

- 1 tablespoon olive oil

- 1 teaspoon ground cumin

- 1 teaspoon ground coriander

- 1/2 teaspoon ground cinnamon

- 1/2 teaspoon ground turmeric

- 1 can chickpeas, rinsed and drained

- 2 carrots, peeled and diced

- 1 sweet potato, peeled and diced

- 1 zucchini, diced

- 1 cup diced tomatoes

- 2 cups vegetable broth
- Salt and pepper to taste
- Fresh cilantro for garnish

Instructions:

1. In a large pot or tagine, sauté onion and garlic in olive oil until softened.
2. Add ground cumin, coriander, cinnamon, and turmeric. Cook for 1 minute until fragrant.
3. Stir in chickpeas, carrots, sweet potato, zucchini, diced tomatoes, and vegetable broth.
4. Bring to a boil, then reduce heat and simmer covered for 30-35 minutes until vegetables are tender.
5. Season with salt and pepper to taste.
6. Garnish with fresh cilantro before serving.

Nutrition Information:

- Calories: 320
- Protein: 10g
- Carbohydrates: 60g
- Fat: 6g
- Fiber: 12g
- Sugar: 12g
- Portion Size: 1/4 of the tagine

Grilled Portobello Mushrooms

Ingredients:

- 4 large portobello mushrooms
- 1/4 cup balsamic vinegar
- 2 tablespoons olive oil
- 2 cloves garlic, minced
- 1 teaspoon dried thyme
- Salt and pepper to taste
- Fresh parsley for garnish

Instructions:

1. Clean mushrooms and remove stems.
2. In a shallow dish, whisk together balsamic vinegar, olive oil, minced garlic, dried thyme, salt, and pepper.
3. Place mushrooms in the marinade, turning to coat. Let marinate for at least 30 minutes.
4. Preheat grill or grill pan over medium heat. Grill mushrooms for 4-5 minutes per side until tender.
5. Serve grilled portobello mushrooms garnished with fresh parsley.

Nutrition Information:

- Calories: 120
- Protein: 5g

- Carbohydrates: 10g
- Fat: 7g
- Fiber: 3g
- Sugar: 5g
- Portion Size: 1 mushroom

Sweet Potato and Lentil Shepherd's Pie

Ingredients:

- 2 large sweet potatoes, peeled and cubed
- 1 cup green lentils, rinsed
- 2 cups vegetable broth
- 1 onion, diced
- 2 carrots, diced
- 2 celery stalks, diced
- 2 cloves garlic, minced
- 1 teaspoon dried thyme
- Salt and pepper to taste
- Fresh parsley for garnish

Instructions:

1. Preheat oven to 375°F (190°C). In a large pot, combine sweet potatoes and enough water to cover. Bring to a boil

and cook until tender, about 15 minutes. Drain and mash with a fork.

2. In another pot, sauté onion, carrots, celery, and garlic until softened.

3. Add green lentils, vegetable broth, dried thyme, salt, and pepper. Bring to a boil, then reduce heat and simmer for 20-25 minutes until lentils are tender and liquid is absorbed.

4. Transfer lentil mixture to a baking dish. Spread mashed sweet potatoes over the top.

5. Bake for 20 minutes until heated through and slightly golden on top.

6. Garnish with fresh parsley before serving.

Nutrition Information:

- Calories: 350
- Protein: 15g
- Carbohydrates: 65g
- Fat: 5g
- Fiber: 15g
- Sugar: 12g
- Portion Size: 1/4 of the pie

Chapter 5: Snacks and Appetizers

In between meals, having nutritious snacks can help maintain energy levels and satisfy hunger. These snacks are not only delicious but also packed with essential nutrients to support your health goals. From protein-packed options to fiber-rich treats, here are snack and appetizer ideas to enjoy throughout your day.

Roasted Chickpeas

Ingredients:

- 1 can (15 oz) chickpeas, drained and rinsed
- 1 tablespoon olive oil
- 1 teaspoon cumin
- 1/2 teaspoon paprika
- Salt to taste

Instructions:

1. Preheat oven to 400°F (200°C).
2. Pat chickpeas dry with a paper towel.
3. Toss chickpeas with olive oil, cumin, paprika, and salt.
4. Spread on a baking sheet and bake for 25-30 minutes, shaking the pan halfway through.
5. Let cool before serving.

Nutrition Information (per serving):

- Calories: 160
- Protein: 6g
- Carbohydrates: 22g
- Fat: 6g
- Fiber: 6g
- Sugar: 4g
- Serving Size: 1/2 cup

Hummus with Carrot Sticks

Ingredients:

- 1 cup hummus
- 4 medium carrots, peeled and cut into sticks

Instructions:

1. Place hummus in a bowl.
2. Arrange carrot sticks around the hummus.
3. Serve immediately.

Nutrition Information (per serving):

- Calories: 150
- Protein: 6g
- Carbohydrates: 20g

- Fat: 7g
- Fiber: 8g
- Sugar: 4g
- Serving Size: 1/2 cup hummus with 1 carrot

Guacamole with Whole Grain Crackers

Ingredients:

- 2 ripe avocados, peeled and mashed
- 1 tomato, diced
- 1/4 cup onion, finely chopped
- 1 tablespoon lime juice
- Salt and pepper to taste
- Whole grain crackers, for serving

Instructions:

1. In a bowl, combine mashed avocados, tomato, onion, lime juice, salt, and pepper.
2. Mix well.
3. Serve with whole grain crackers.

Nutrition Information (per serving, guacamole only):

- Calories: 120
- Protein: 2g

- Carbohydrates: 8g
- Fat: 10g
- Fiber: 6g
- Sugar: 1g
- Serving Size: 1/4 cup guacamole

Greek Yogurt with Fresh Berries

Ingredients:

- 1 cup Greek yogurt
- 1/2 cup fresh berries (such as strawberries, blueberries, raspberries)

Instructions:

1. Spoon Greek yogurt into a bowl.
2. Top with fresh berries.
3. Serve immediately.

Nutrition Information (per serving):

- Calories: 150
- Protein: 15g
- Carbohydrates: 20g
- Fat: 0g
- Fiber: 3g

- Sugar: 15g
- Serving Size: 1 cup yogurt with 1/2 cup berries

Apple Slices with Peanut Butter

Ingredients:

- 1 medium apple, sliced
- 2 tablespoons peanut butter

Instructions:

1. Slice the apple into wedges.
2. Spread peanut butter on each slice.
3. Arrange on a plate and serve.

Nutrition Information (per serving):

- Calories: 200
- Protein: 7g
- Carbohydrates: 25g
- Fat: 10g
- Fiber: 5g
- Sugar: 15g
- Serving Size: 1 medium apple with 2 tablespoons peanut butter

Celery Sticks with Almond Butter

Ingredients:

- 4 celery stalks, cut into sticks
- 1/4 cup almond butter

Instructions:

1. Spread almond butter into celery sticks.
2. Arrange on a plate and serve.

Nutrition Information (per serving):

- Calories: 180
- Protein: 6g
- Carbohydrates: 10g
- Fat: 14g
- Fiber: 4g
- Sugar: 3g
- Serving Size: 4 celery sticks with 1/4 cup almond butter

Mixed Nuts and Seeds

Ingredients:

- 1/4 cup mixed nuts (such as almonds, walnuts, cashews)
- 1 tablespoon mixed seeds (such as pumpkin seeds, sunflower seeds)

Instructions:

1. Combine mixed nuts and seeds in a bowl.

2. Toss lightly.

3. Serve in a small bowl.

Nutrition Information (per serving):

- Calories: 200
- Protein: 7g
- Carbohydrates: 8g
- Fat: 15g
- Fiber: 4g
- Sugar: 1g
- Serving Size: 1/4 cup mixed nuts and 1 tablespoon seeds

Edamame with Sea Salt

Ingredients:

- 1 cup edamame (frozen or fresh)
- Sea salt, to taste

Instructions:

1. Cook edamame according to package instructions.

2. Drain and sprinkle with sea salt.

3. Serve warm or chilled.

Nutrition Information (per serving):

- Calories: 120
- Protein: 11g
- Carbohydrates: 10g
- Fat: 4g
- Fiber: 6g
- Sugar: 3g
- Serving Size: 1 cup edamame

Baked Kale Chips

Ingredients:

- 1 bunch kale, washed and dried
- 1 tablespoon olive oil
- Salt and pepper, to taste

Instructions:

1. Preheat oven to 300°F (150°C).
2. Remove kale leaves from stems and tear into bite-sized pieces.
3. Toss kale with olive oil, salt, and pepper.
4. Spread on a baking sheet in a single layer.
5. Bake for 10-15 minutes until crispy.
6. Let cool before serving.

Nutrition Information (per serving):

- Calories: 50
- Protein: 2g
- Carbohydrates: 5g
- Fat: 3g
- Fiber: 1g
- Sugar: 0g
- Serving Size: 1 cup kale chips

Stuffed Mini Bell Peppers

Ingredients:

- 12 mini bell peppers, halved and seeds removed
- 1 cup cottage cheese
- 1/4 cup chopped fresh herbs (such as parsley or chives)

Instructions:

1. In a bowl, mix cottage cheese and chopped herbs.
2. Stuff each mini bell pepper half with the cottage cheese mixture.
3. Arrange on a serving platter and serve chilled.

Nutrition Information (per serving):

- Calories: 80

- Protein: 8g
- Carbohydrates: 10g
- Fat: 2g
- Fiber: 2g
- Sugar: 6g
- Serving Size: 4 stuffed mini bell pepper halves

Spicy Roasted Almonds

Ingredients:
- 1 cup raw almonds
- 1 tablespoon olive oil
- 1 teaspoon smoked paprika
- 1/2 teaspoon cayenne pepper
- Salt, to taste

Instructions:
1. Preheat oven to 350°F (175°C).
2. In a bowl, toss almonds with olive oil, smoked paprika, cayenne pepper, and salt.
3. Spread almonds on a baking sheet in a single layer.
4. Roast for 12-15 minutes, stirring halfway through.
5. Let cool before serving.

Nutrition Information (per serving):

- Calories: 180
- Protein: 6g
- Carbohydrates: 6g
- Fat: 15g
- Fiber: 3g
- Sugar: 1g
- Serving Size: 1/4 cup almonds

Cottage Cheese with Cucumber Slices

Ingredients:

- 1 cup low-fat cottage cheese
- 1 cucumber, sliced

Instructions:

1. Spoon cottage cheese into a bowl.
2. Arrange cucumber slices around the cottage cheese.
3. Serve chilled.

Nutrition Information (per serving):

- Calories: 120
- Protein: 15g
- Carbohydrates: 10g

- Fat: 2g
- Fiber: 1g
- Sugar: 6g
- Serving Size: 1 cup cottage cheese with 1 cucumber

Berry and Nut Mix

Ingredients:
- 1/2 cup mixed berries (such as strawberries, blueberries, raspberries)
- 1/4 cup mixed nuts (such as almonds, walnuts, pecans)

Instructions:
1. Combine mixed berries and nuts in a bowl.
2. Toss lightly.
3. Serve in a small bowl.

Nutrition Information (per serving):
- Calories: 150
- Protein: 5g
- Carbohydrates: 15g
- Fat: 9g
- Fiber: 4g
- Sugar: 8g

- Serving Size: 1/2 cup mix

Sliced Avocado with Lime

Ingredients:

- 1 ripe avocado, sliced
- 1 lime, cut into wedges

Instructions:

1. Arrange avocado slices on a plate.
2. Squeeze lime juice over the avocado slices.
3. Serve immediately.

Nutrition Information (per serving):

- Calories: 160
- Protein: 2g
- Carbohydrates: 9g
- Fat: 15g
- Fiber: 7g
- Sugar: 1g
- Serving Size: 1/2 avocado with juice of 1 lime

Tomato and Basil Bruschetta

Ingredients:

- 4 slices whole grain baguette, toasted
- 2 tomatoes, diced
- 1/4 cup fresh basil leaves, chopped
- 1 clove garlic, minced
- 1 tablespoon balsamic vinegar
- Salt and pepper, to taste

Instructions:

1. In a bowl, combine diced tomatoes, chopped basil, minced garlic, balsamic vinegar, salt, and pepper.
2. Spoon tomato mixture evenly onto toasted baguette slices.
3. Serve immediately.

Nutrition Information (per serving, 1 slice of bruschetta):

- Calories: 80
- Protein: 3g
- Carbohydrates: 15g
- Fat: 1g
- Fiber: 2g
- Sugar: 3g
- Serving Size: 1 slice

Chapter 6: Desserts

Indulge in these delightful desserts that are not only delicious but also tailored to support your vegetarian diet aimed at managing pre-diabetes and high cholesterol. Each recipe focuses on wholesome ingredients and simple preparation methods, ensuring both taste and health benefits.

Chia Seed Pudding with Fresh Berries

Ingredients:

- 1/4 cup chia seeds
- 1 cup almond milk
- 1 tablespoon maple syrup (optional)
- Fresh berries for topping

Instructions:

1. Mix chia seeds, almond milk, and maple syrup in a bowl.
2. Stir well and refrigerate overnight or for at least 4 hours.
3. Serve topped with fresh berries.

Nutrition Information (per serving):

- Calories: 180
- Protein: 5g

- Carbohydrates: 25g
- Fat: 7g
- Fiber: 10g
- Sugar: 8g
- Portion Size: 1 cup

Baked Pears with Cinnamon

Ingredients:

- 4 ripe pears, halved and cored
- 1 tablespoon honey
- 1 teaspoon cinnamon

Instructions:

1. Preheat oven to 375°F (190°C).
2. Place pears on a baking sheet, cut side up.
3. Drizzle with honey and sprinkle with cinnamon.
4. Bake for 25-30 minutes until tender.
5. Serve warm.

Nutrition Information (per serving):

- Calories: 120
- Protein: 1g
- Carbohydrates: 32g

- Fat: 0.5g
- Fiber: 6g
- Sugar: 24g
- Portion Size: 1 pear half

Dark Chocolate and Almond Clusters

Ingredients:
- 1 cup dark chocolate chips
- 1 cup almonds, chopped

Instructions:
1. Melt dark chocolate chips in a microwave-safe bowl in 30-second intervals, stirring in between.
2. Stir in chopped almonds until well coated.
3. Drop spoonfuls of the mixture onto a parchment-lined baking sheet.
4. Let cool until chocolate hardens.
5. Enjoy as clusters.

Nutrition Information (per serving):
- Calories: 180
- Protein: 4g
- Carbohydrates: 15g

- Fat: 12g
- Fiber: 3g
- Sugar: 10g
- Portion Size: 2 clusters

Mango Sorbet

Ingredients:
- 2 cups frozen mango chunks
- 1/4 cup coconut milk
- 1 tablespoon honey (optional)

Instructions:
1. Blend frozen mango chunks, coconut milk, and honey in a blender until smooth.
2. Serve immediately as soft-serve or freeze for 1-2 hours for a firmer texture.
3. Garnish with fresh mango slices if desired.

Nutrition Information (per serving):
- Calories: 150
- Protein: 1g
- Carbohydrates: 35g
- Fat: 2g

- Fiber: 3g
- Sugar: 30g
- Portion Size: 1 cup

Apple Crisp with Oats

Ingredients:

- 4 apples, peeled, cored, and sliced
- 1 tablespoon lemon juice
- 1/2 cup rolled oats
- 1/4 cup whole wheat flour
- 1/4 cup coconut sugar
- 1/4 cup melted coconut oil
- 1 teaspoon cinnamon

Instructions:

1. Preheat oven to 350°F (175°C).
2. Toss apple slices with lemon juice and place in a baking dish.
3. In a bowl, combine oats, flour, coconut sugar, melted coconut oil, and cinnamon until crumbly.
4. Sprinkle oat mixture evenly over apples.
5. Bake for 30-35 minutes until topping is golden brown and apples are tender.
6. Serve warm.

Nutrition Information (per serving):

- Calories: 250
- Protein: 3g
- Carbohydrates: 40g
- Fat: 10g
- Fiber: 6g
- Sugar: 25g
- Portion Size: 1/6 of the dish

Blueberry Almond Parfait

Ingredients:

- 1 cup Greek yogurt
- 1 cup fresh blueberries
- 1/4 cup almonds, chopped
- 1 tablespoon honey or maple syrup (optional)

Instructions:

1. Layer Greek yogurt, blueberries, and chopped almonds in a glass or bowl.
2. Drizzle with honey or maple syrup if desired.
3. Repeat layers.
4. Serve chilled.

Nutrition Information (per serving):

- Calories: 200
- Protein: 10g
- Carbohydrates: 25g
- Fat: 7g
- Fiber: 4g
- Sugar: 18g
- Portion Size: 1 cup

Vegan Banana Bread

Ingredients:

- 3 ripe bananas, mashed
- 1/4 cup coconut oil, melted
- 1/2 cup coconut sugar
- 1 teaspoon vanilla extract
- 1 1/2 cups whole wheat flour
- 1 teaspoon baking soda
- 1/2 teaspoon salt
- 1/2 teaspoon cinnamon
- 1/4 cup almond milk (or any plant-based milk)

Instructions:

1. Preheat oven to 350°F (175°C). Grease a loaf pan.

2. In a large bowl, mix mashed bananas, coconut oil, coconut sugar, and vanilla extract.

3. In another bowl, whisk together whole wheat flour, baking soda, salt, and cinnamon.

4. Gradually add dry ingredients to wet ingredients, alternating with almond milk, until combined.

5. Pour batter into the prepared loaf pan.

6. Bake for 50-60 minutes or until a toothpick inserted into the center comes out clean.

7. Allow to cool before slicing.

Nutrition Information (per serving):

- Calories: 220
- Protein: 3g
- Carbohydrates: 35g
- Fat: 9g
- Fiber: 3g
- Sugar: 16g
- Portion Size: 1 slice

Coconut Milk Ice Cream

Ingredients:

- 1 can (14 oz) coconut milk

- 1/4 cup maple syrup or agave syrup
- 1 teaspoon vanilla extract
- Pinch of salt

Instructions:

1. Chill the coconut milk in the refrigerator overnight.
2. In a bowl, whisk together chilled coconut milk, maple syrup, vanilla extract, and salt.
3. Pour mixture into an ice cream maker and churn according to manufacturer's instructions.
4. Transfer churned ice cream to a container and freeze for 2-3 hours until firm.
5. Serve scoops of coconut milk ice cream.

Nutrition Information (per serving):

- Calories: 250
- Protein: 2g
- Carbohydrates: 20g
- Fat: 19g
- Fiber: 1g
- Sugar: 15g
- Portion Size: 1/2 cup

Pumpkin Pie with Almond Crust

Ingredients:

For the almond crust:

- 1 cup almond flour
- 1/4 cup melted coconut oil
- 1 tablespoon maple syrup

For the pumpkin filling:

- 1 can (15 oz) pumpkin puree
- 1/2 cup coconut milk
- 1/3 cup coconut sugar
- 2 tablespoons cornstarch
- 1 teaspoon vanilla extract
- 1 teaspoon ground cinnamon
- 1/2 teaspoon ground ginger
- 1/4 teaspoon ground nutmeg
- Pinch of salt

Instructions:

1. Preheat oven to 350°F (175°C).
2. In a bowl, combine almond flour, melted coconut oil, and maple syrup. Press mixture into a pie dish to form the crust.

3. In another bowl, whisk together pumpkin puree, coconut milk, coconut sugar, cornstarch, vanilla extract, cinnamon, ginger, nutmeg, and salt until smooth.
4. Pour pumpkin filling into the almond crust.
5. Bake for 50-55 minutes or until set.
6. Allow to cool before slicing and serving.

Nutrition Information (per serving):
- Calories: 280
- Protein: 4g
- Carbohydrates: 30g
- Fat: 17g
- Fiber: 5g
- Sugar: 15g
- Portion Size: 1/8 of the pie

Raspberry Chia Jam Bars

Ingredients:

For the raspberry chia jam:
- 2 cups fresh raspberries
- 2 tablespoons chia seeds
- 2 tablespoons maple syrup

For the oat crumble:

- 1 cup rolled oats
- 1/2 cup almond flour
- 1/4 cup coconut oil, melted
- 1/4 cup coconut sugar
- 1/2 teaspoon vanilla extract
- Pinch of salt

Instructions:

1. Preheat oven to 350°F (175°C). Grease a baking dish.
2. In a saucepan, heat raspberries over medium heat until they break down, about 5 minutes.
3. Stir in chia seeds and maple syrup. Cook for another 5 minutes until thickened. Remove from heat and let cool.
4. In a bowl, combine rolled oats, almond flour, melted coconut oil, coconut sugar, vanilla extract, and salt. Mix until crumbly.
5. Press half of the oat mixture into the bottom of the greased baking dish.
6. Spread raspberry chia jam evenly over the oat layer.
7. Sprinkle remaining oat mixture over the jam layer.
8. Bake for 25-30 minutes or until golden brown.
9. Allow to cool completely before cutting into bars.

Nutrition Information (per serving):

- Calories: 220
- Protein: 4g
- Carbohydrates: 30g
- Fat: 10g
- Fiber: 6g
- Sugar: 12g
- Portion Size: 1 bar

Avocado Chocolate Mousse

Ingredients:

- 2 ripe avocados
- 1/4 cup cocoa powder
- 1/4 cup maple syrup or agave syrup
- 1 teaspoon vanilla extract
- Pinch of salt
- Optional toppings: shaved dark chocolate, berries

Instructions:

1. Scoop out the flesh of the avocados and place in a food processor.
2. Add cocoa powder, maple syrup or agave syrup, vanilla extract, and a pinch of salt.

3. Blend until smooth and creamy, scraping down the sides as needed.

4. Divide into serving dishes and chill in the refrigerator for at least 30 minutes.

5. Serve topped with shaved dark chocolate and berries if desired.

Nutrition Information (per serving):
- Calories: 200
- Protein: 3g
- Carbohydrates: 20g
- Fat: 15g
- Fiber: 7g
- Sugar: 10g
- Portion Size: 1/2 cup

Poached Pears with Spices

Ingredients:
- 4 ripe pears, peeled and halved
- 2 cups water
- 1/2 cup honey or maple syrup
- 1 cinnamon stick
- 1 star anise

- 1 teaspoon vanilla extract

Instructions:

1. In a large saucepan, combine water, honey or maple syrup, cinnamon stick, star anise, and vanilla extract. Bring to a simmer.
2. Add pear halves to the simmering liquid. Cover and cook for 15-20 minutes, turning occasionally, until pears are tender.
3. Remove pears from liquid and let cool slightly.
4. Serve warm or chilled, drizzled with a little of the poaching liquid.

Nutrition Information (per serving):

- Calories: 180
- Protein: 1g
- Carbohydrates: 45g
- Fat: 0.5g
- Fiber: 5g
- Sugar: 35g
- Portion Size: 1 pear half

Lemon Sorbet

Ingredients:

- 1 cup fresh lemon juice (from about 6 lemons)
- 1 cup water
- 3/4 cup granulated sugar
- Zest of 1 lemon

Instructions:

1. In a saucepan, combine water and sugar. Heat over medium heat, stirring until sugar dissolves.
2. Remove from heat and stir in fresh lemon juice and lemon zest.
3. Pour mixture into a shallow dish and freeze for 4-6 hours, stirring every hour with a fork to break up ice crystals.
4. Serve lemon sorbet scooped into bowls or glasses.

Nutrition Information (per serving):

- Calories: 120
- Protein: 0g
- Carbohydrates: 32g
- Fat: 0g
- Fiber: 0g
- Sugar: 30g
- Portion Size: 1/2 cup

Strawberry Basil Popsicles

Ingredients:

- 2 cups fresh strawberries, hulled and chopped
- 1/4 cup fresh basil leaves, chopped
- 1/4 cup honey or maple syrup
- 1 cup coconut water or water

Instructions:

1. In a blender, combine strawberries, basil leaves, honey or maple syrup, and coconut water or water.
2. Blend until smooth.
3. Pour mixture into popsicle molds.
4. Insert sticks and freeze for at least 4 hours or until firm.
5. Run molds under warm water briefly to release popsicles before serving.

Nutrition Information (per popsicle):

- Calories: 50
- Protein: 0.5g
- Carbohydrates: 12g
- Fat: 0g
- Fiber: 1g
- Sugar: 10g
- Portion Size: 1 popsicle

Sweet Potato Brownies

Ingredients:

- 2 cups mashed sweet potatoes (about 2 medium sweet potatoes)
- 1/2 cup almond butter
- 1/4 cup maple syrup
- 1/4 cup cocoa powder
- 1 teaspoon vanilla extract
- 1/2 teaspoon baking soda
- 1/4 teaspoon salt
- 1/2 cup dark chocolate chips (optional)

Instructions:

1. Preheat oven to 350°F (175°C). Grease a baking dish or line with parchment paper.
2. In a bowl, combine mashed sweet potatoes, almond butter, maple syrup, cocoa powder, vanilla extract, baking soda, and salt. Mix until smooth.
3. Fold in dark chocolate chips if using.
4. Spread batter evenly into the prepared baking dish.
5. Bake for 25-30 minutes or until edges are set and a toothpick inserted into the center comes out clean.
6. Allow to cool before slicing into squares.

Nutrition Information (per serving):

- Calories: 180
- Protein: 4g
- Carbohydrates: 25g
- Fat: 8g
- Fiber: 4g
- Sugar: 12g
- Portion Size: 1 brownie

Chapter 7: Smoothies

Smoothies are a delicious and convenient way to pack nutrients into your day, whether as a quick breakfast, a post-workout refuel, or a refreshing snack. These recipes are designed to be easy to prepare and full of wholesome ingredients to support your health goals. Each smoothie is packed with flavor and nutritional benefits to keep you energized throughout the day.

Green Detox Smoothie

Ingredients:

- 1 cup spinach leaves
- 1/2 cucumber, chopped
- 1/2 green apple, chopped
- 1/2 lemon, juiced
- 1/2 inch piece of ginger, peeled
- 1 cup coconut water
- Ice cubes (optional)

Instructions:

1. Blend all ingredients until smooth.
2. Add ice cubes if desired for a colder smoothie.

Nutrition Information (per serving):

- Calories: 90
- Protein: 2g
- Carbohydrates: 20g
- Fat: 0.5g
- Fiber: 4g
- Sugar: 12g
- Portion size: 1 smoothie

Berry Blast Smoothie

Ingredients:

- 1 cup mixed berries (strawberries, blueberries, raspberries)
- 1/2 cup plain Greek yogurt
- 1 tablespoon honey (optional)
- 1/2 cup almond milk
- Ice cubes

Instructions:

1. Blend berries, Greek yogurt, honey (if using), and almond milk until smooth.
2. Add ice cubes and blend until desired consistency is reached.

Nutrition Information (per serving):

- Calories: 150
- Protein: 7g
- Carbohydrates: 30g
- Fat: 2g
- Fiber: 5g
- Sugar: 20g
- Portion size: 1 smoothie

Tropical Mango Smoothie

Ingredients:

- 1 cup frozen mango chunks
- 1/2 cup pineapple chunks
- 1/2 banana
- 1/2 cup coconut water or coconut milk
- Juice of 1/2 lime
- Ice cubes (optional)

Instructions:

1. Blend mango, pineapple, banana, coconut water or milk, and lime juice until smooth.
2. Add ice cubes if a colder smoothie is desired.

Nutrition Information (per serving):

- Calories: 180
- Protein: 2g
- Carbohydrates: 40g
- Fat: 1g
- Fiber: 5g
- Sugar: 30g
- Portion size: 1 smoothie

Avocado and Spinach Smoothie

Ingredients:

- 1/2 ripe avocado
- 1 cup spinach leaves
- 1/2 cup plain Greek yogurt
- 1 tablespoon honey or maple syrup (optional)
- 1/2 cup almond milk
- Ice cubes

Instructions:

1. Blend avocado, spinach, Greek yogurt, honey or maple syrup (if using), and almond milk until smooth.
2. Add ice cubes and blend until creamy.

Nutrition Information (per serving):

- Calories: 200
- Protein: 8g
- Carbohydrates: 20g
- Fat: 10g
- Fiber: 5g
- Sugar: 10g
- Portion size: 1 smoothie

Peanut Butter Banana Smoothie

Ingredients:

- 1 banana
- 2 tablespoons peanut butter
- 1 cup almond milk
- 1 tablespoon honey or maple syrup (optional)
- Ice cubes

Instructions:

1. Blend banana, peanut butter, almond milk, and honey or maple syrup (if using) until smooth.
2. Add ice cubes and blend until well combined.

Nutrition Information (per serving):

- Calories: 300
- Protein: 8g
- Carbohydrates: 30g
- Fat: 18g
- Fiber: 5g
- Sugar: 15g
- Portion size: 1 smoothie

Almond and Date Smoothie

Ingredients:

- 1/4 cup almonds, soaked overnight
- 4-5 pitted dates
- 1 cup almond milk
- 1/2 teaspoon vanilla extract
- Ice cubes

Instructions:

1. Blend soaked almonds, dates, almond milk, and vanilla extract until smooth.
2. Add ice cubes and blend until creamy.

Nutrition Information (per serving):

- Calories: 250
- Protein: 7g
- Carbohydrates: 30g
- Fat: 12g
- Fiber: 6g
- Sugar: 20g
- Portion size: 1 smoothie

Blueberry and Oat Smoothie

Ingredients:

- 1 cup blueberries (fresh or frozen)
- 1/2 cup rolled oats
- 1/2 cup plain Greek yogurt
- 1 tablespoon honey or maple syrup (optional)
- 1 cup almond milk
- Ice cubes

Instructions:

1. Blend blueberries, oats, Greek yogurt, honey or maple syrup (if using), and almond milk until smooth.
2. Add ice cubes and blend until well combined.

Nutrition Information (per serving):

- Calories: 250
- Protein: 10g
- Carbohydrates: 40g
- Fat: 5g
- Fiber: 6g
- Sugar: 20g
- Portion size: 1 smoothie

Kale and Pineapple Smoothie

Ingredients:

- 1 cup kale leaves, stems removed
- 1 cup pineapple chunks
- 1/2 banana
- 1 tablespoon chia seeds
- 1/2 cup coconut water or almond milk
- Ice cubes

Instructions:

1. Blend kale, pineapple, banana, chia seeds, and coconut water or almond milk until smooth.
2. Add ice cubes and blend until desired consistency is reached.

Nutrition Information (per serving):

- Calories: 180
- Protein: 5g
- Carbohydrates: 35g
- Fat: 3g
- Fiber: 8g
- Sugar: 20g
- Portion size: 1 smoothie

Carrot and Ginger Smoothie

Ingredients:

- 1 cup carrots, chopped
- 1/2 inch piece of ginger, peeled
- 1/2 cup orange juice
- 1/2 cup plain Greek yogurt
- 1 tablespoon honey or maple syrup (optional)
- Ice cubes

Instructions:

1. Blend carrots, ginger, orange juice, Greek yogurt, and honey or maple syrup (if using) until smooth.
2. Add ice cubes and blend until well incorporated.

Nutrition Information (per serving):

- Calories: 150
- Protein: 7g
- Carbohydrates: 30g
- Fat: 1g
- Fiber: 5g
- Sugar: 20g
- Portion size: 1 smoothie

Apple Cinnamon Smoothie

Ingredients:

- 1 apple, cored and chopped
- 1/2 teaspoon ground cinnamon
- 1/2 cup rolled oats
- 1/2 cup almond milk
- 1 tablespoon honey or maple syrup (optional)
- Ice cubes

Instructions:

1. Blend apple, cinnamon, rolled oats, almond milk, and honey or maple syrup (if using) until smooth.
2. Add ice cubes and blend until well combined.

Nutrition Information (per serving):

- Calories: 200
- Protein: 5g
- Carbohydrates: 40g
- Fat: 3g
- Fiber: 7g
- Sugar: 15g
- Portion size: 1 smoothie

Choco-Berry Smoothie

Ingredients:

- 1 cup mixed berries (strawberries, raspberries, blueberries)
- 1 tablespoon cocoa powder
- 1/2 banana
- 1 cup almond milk
- 1 tablespoon honey or maple syrup (optional)
- Ice cubes

Instructions:

1. Blend mixed berries, cocoa powder, banana, almond milk, and honey or maple syrup (if using) until smooth.
2. Add ice cubes and blend until creamy.

Nutrition Information (per serving):

- Calories: 180
- Protein: 5g
- Carbohydrates: 35g
- Fat: 4g
- Fiber: 8g
- Sugar: 20g
- Portion size: 1 smoothie

Coconut and Berry Smoothie

Ingredients:

- 1/2 cup mixed berries (strawberries, raspberries, blueberries)
- 1/2 cup coconut milk
- 1/2 cup plain Greek yogurt
- 1 tablespoon shredded coconut (optional)
- Ice cubes

Instructions:

1. Blend mixed berries, coconut milk, Greek yogurt, and shredded coconut (if using) until smooth.
2. Add ice cubes and blend until desired consistency is reached.

Nutrition Information (per serving):

- Calories: 220
- Protein: 8g
- Carbohydrates: 25g
- Fat: 12g
- Fiber: 5g
- Sugar: 15g
- Portion size: 1 smoothie

Beetroot and Orange Smoothie

Ingredients:

- 1 small beetroot, peeled and chopped
- Juice of 2 oranges
- 1/2 cup plain Greek yogurt
- 1 tablespoon honey or maple syrup (optional)
- Ice cubes

Instructions:

1. Blend beetroot, orange juice, Greek yogurt, and honey or maple syrup (if using) until smooth.
2. Add ice cubes and blend until well combined.

Nutrition Information (per serving):

- Calories: 160
- Protein: 7g
- Carbohydrates: 30g
- Fat: 1g
- Fiber: 5g
- Sugar: 25g
- Portion size: 1 smoothie

Strawberry and Mint Smoothie

Ingredients:

- 1 cup strawberries, hulled
- 1/4 cup fresh mint leaves
- 1/2 cup plain Greek yogurt
- 1 tablespoon honey or maple syrup (optional)
- 1/2 cup almond milk
- Ice cubes

Instructions:

1. Blend strawberries, mint leaves, Greek yogurt, honey or maple syrup (if using), and almond milk until smooth.
2. Add ice cubes and blend until creamy.

Nutrition Information (per serving):

- Calories: 140
- Protein: 6g
- Carbohydrates: 25g
- Fat: 2g
- Fiber: 5g
- Sugar: 20g
- Portion size: 1 smoothie

Pumpkin Spice Smoothie

Ingredients:

- 1/2 cup pumpkin puree
- 1/2 banana
- 1/2 teaspoon pumpkin pie spice
- 1 cup almond milk
- 1 tablespoon maple syrup
- Ice cubes

Instructions:

1. Blend pumpkin puree, banana, pumpkin pie spice, almond milk, and maple syrup until smooth.
2. Add ice cubes and blend until well combined.

Nutrition Information (per serving):

- Calories: 180
- Protein: 4g
- Carbohydrates: 35g
- Fat: 4g
- Fiber: 8g
- Sugar: 20g
- Portion size: 1 smoothie

CONCLUSION

Congratulations on completing your journey through the "Vegetarian Meal Plan for Beginners with Pre-Diabetes and High Cholesterol"! This book has been crafted to empower you with delicious, nutritious recipes and valuable insights to support your health goals.

Throughout these pages, you've explored the vibrant world of vegetarian cuisine, discovering flavorful dishes that not only delight the taste buds but also contribute to managing pre-diabetes and high cholesterol. By focusing on wholesome ingredients rich in fiber, vitamins, and plant-based proteins, you've equipped yourself with tools to nurture your well-being.

Remember, adopting a vegetarian diet isn't just about what you eat; it's about embracing a sustainable lifestyle that supports long-term health. Whether you're enjoying a hearty breakfast, a satisfying lunch, or a delightful dessert, each recipe has been carefully selected to provide balanced nutrition and culinary enjoyment.

As you continue your journey beyond these recipes, keep experimenting with flavors, ingredients, and cooking techniques that inspire you. Stay mindful of your dietary choices and listen to your body's needs. Small changes today can lead to significant health improvements tomorrow.

Thank you for embarking on this transformative journey with us. May your path be filled with health, vitality, and the joy of delicious vegetarian meals. Here's to a vibrant future filled with good food and great health!

Made in the USA
Monee, IL
20 October 2024

68321091R00075